Professor Pete's Prehistoric Animals

LONG -NECKED DINOSAURS

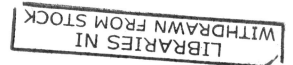

W

FRANKLIN WATTS
LONDON•SYDNEY

Franklin Watts
This edition published in the UK in 2017 by The Watts Publishing Group

Copyright © 2013 David West Children's Books

All rights reserved.

Designed and illustrated by David West

ISBN 978 1 4451 5502 9

Printed in Malaysia

Franklin Watts
An imprint of
Hachette Children's Group
Part of The Watts Publishing Group
Carmelite House
50 Victoria Embankment
London EC4Y 0DZ

An Hachette UK Company.
www.hachette.co.uk

www.franklinwatts.co.uk

PROFESSOR PETE'S PREHISTORIC ANIMALS LONG-NECKED DINOSAURS
was produced for Franklin Watts by
David West Children's Books, 6 Princeton Court, 55 Felsham Road, London SW15 1AZ

Professor Pete says:
This little guy will tell you something more about the animal.

Learn what this animal ate.

Where and when (Mya=Millions of Years Ago) did it live?

Its size is revealed!

How fast or slow was it?

Discover the meaning of its name.

A timeline on page 24 shows you the dates of the different periods in Mya.

Contents

Amargasaurus 4

Antarctosaurus 6

Brachiosaurus 8

Brachytrachelopan 10

Diamantinasaurus 12

Diplodocus 14

Europasaurus 16

Mamenchisaurus 18

Spinophorosaurus 20

Uberabatitan 22

Glossary and Timeline 24

Amargasaurus

a-MARG-oh-sore-us

Amargasaurus was a strange-looking **sauropod**. It had tall spine bones along its back and neck giving it a double hump appearance.

Amargasaurus was a plant-eating dinosaur.

It lived in Argentina during the Lower Cretaceous period, 132–127 Mya.

Amargasaurus was about 12 metres long and weighed 5 tonnes.

Amargasaurus could probably run as fast as 20 kilometres per hour.

Amargasaurus means 'the Amarga lizard' after the Amarga creek close to where it was found.

Professor Pete says:
Nobody knows why Amargasaurus had a double hump. It may have helped it to look bigger to scare off meat-eating dinosaurs.

5

Professor Pete says:
Fully grown, Antarctosaurus did not have to worry about **predators**. It was far too big even for the massive, meat-eating Abelisaurus.

Antarctosaurus

ant-ARK-toe-sore-us

This huge herbivore lived in South America. It was one of the largest land animals ever to have walked the Earth.

 Antarctosaurus was a plant eater. It probably fed on the needle leaves of tall conifer trees.

It lived in Argentina, Chile and Uruguay during the Upper Cretaceous period, 87–85 Mya.

 Antarctosaurus grew up to more than 24.4 metres long and weighed a huge 55–73 tonnes!

 Like all sauropods it moved at a slow pace, reaching top speeds of less than 16 kilometres per hour.

Antarctosaurus means 'southern lizard'.

Brachiosaurus

BRAK-ee-oh-sore-us

Unlike most sauropods, Brachiosaurus had a giraffe-like build. Its front legs were longer than its back legs. It could rear up on its back legs to reach leaves on higher branches.

Professor Pete says:
Brachiosaurus needed to eat huge amounts of vegetation. Scientists have worked out that it would have eaten more than 182 kilogrammes of plants daily.

Brachiosaurus means 'arm lizard' because its front 'arm' limbs were longer than its back limbs.

Brachiosaurus could only run up to 24.1 kilometres per hour.

Brachiosaurus was about 25 metres in length and weighed around 70 metric tonnes.

It lived in Europe, Africa and North America during the Upper Jurassic/Lower Cretaceous periods, 155–140 Mya.

Brachiosaurus was a plant eater and fed on the leaves of the tallest trees.

Brachytrachelopan

brak-i-trak-eh-loh-pan

This member of the long-necked dinosaur family was the exception that proved the rule. Its neck was half as long as other sauropods from the Jurassic period.

It was a plant eater and probably fed on plants that grew a few feet from the ground.

Brachytrachelopan was about 10 metres in length and weighed around 4.5 tonnes.

It is unlikely that this dinosaur could run much faster than 24.1 kilometres per hour.

Brachytrachelopan means 'short-necked shepherd', because of its short neck and because it was a shepherd who found its fossils.

Brachytrachelopan lived
in Argentina during the
Upper Jurassic period,
150 Mya.

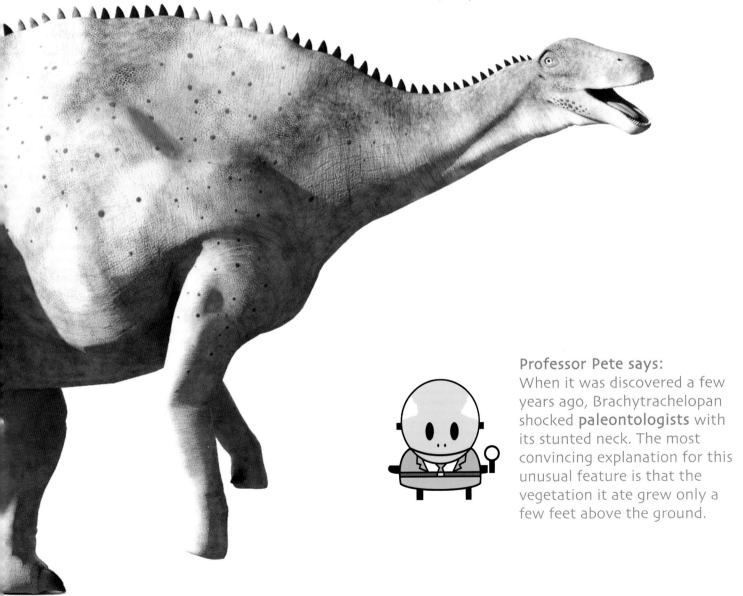

Professor Pete says:
When it was discovered a few
years ago, Brachytrachelopan
shocked **paleontologists** with
its stunted neck. The most
convincing explanation for this
unusual feature is that the
vegetation it ate grew only a
few feet above the ground.

Diamantinasaurus

dee-ah-man-teen-ah-SORE-us

This giant sauropod was a member of the **titanosaur** family. Compared with other titanosaurs this one was relatively small.

Diamantinasaurus was a plant eater but it is not known which plants it ate.

Diamantinasaurus was about 16 metres long and weighed 20 tonnes.

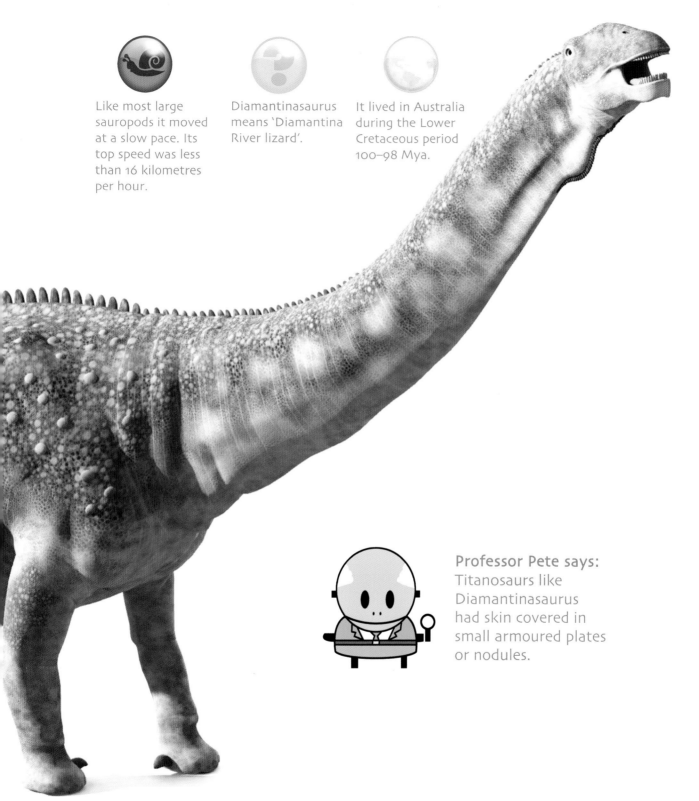

Like most large sauropods it moved at a slow pace. Its top speed was less than 16 kilometres per hour.

Diamantinasaurus means 'Diamantina River lizard'.

It lived in Australia during the Lower Cretaceous period 100–98 Mya.

Professor Pete says:
Titanosaurs like Diamantinasaurus had skin covered in small armoured plates or nodules.

13

Diplodocus

DIP-low-DOCK-us

Diplodocus is one of the longest dinosaurs ever found. Its tail had up to 90 bones. It may have used it like a whip, cracking it to scare away predators.

Diplodocus means 'double beam' due to the double-beamed bones along the underside of its tail.

 Diplodocus was a plant eater. Its long neck allowed it to feed on the soft horsetails, club mosses and ferns.

 It lived in the United States during the Upper Jurassic period, 155–145 Mya.

 Diplodocus was about 27 metres in length and weighed 21.8 tonnes.

 The fastest speed Diplodocus could manage was a slow 14.4 kilometres per hour.

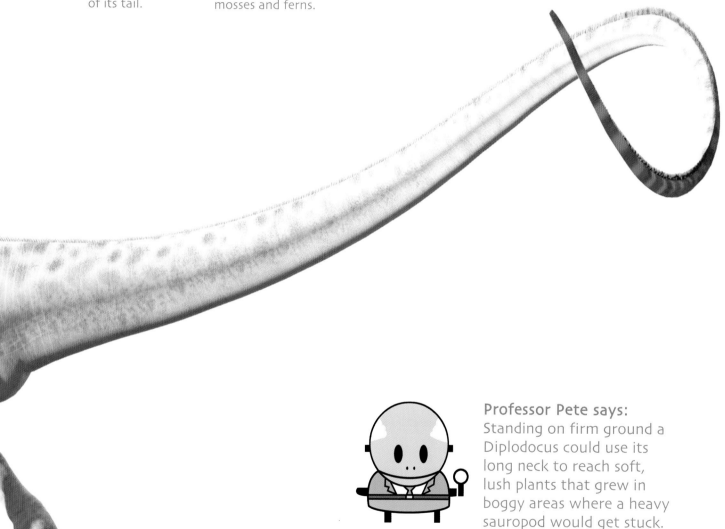

Professor Pete says:
Standing on firm ground a Diplodocus could use its long neck to reach soft, lush plants that grew in boggy areas where a heavy sauropod would get stuck.

Europasaurus

yoo-roh-pah-sore-rus

Not much bigger than an ox, this little dinosaur was a dwarf species of sauropod. Although it evolved from large ancestors it seems that Europasaurus became isolated on islands where there wasn't enough food to support giant dinosaurs.

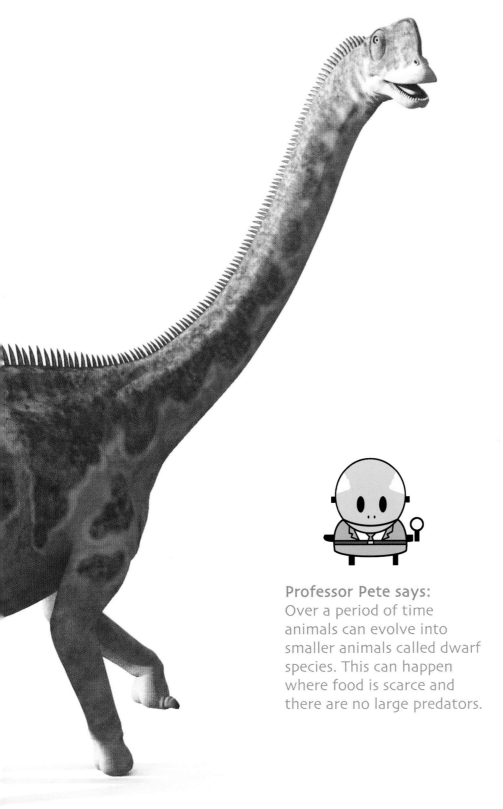

Europasaurus means 'European lizard'.

Europasaurus might have run up to 24.1 kilometres per hour.

Europasaurus was about 5.8 metres in length and weighed around 0.9 tonnes.

It lived in Germany during the Upper Jurassic period, 154–151 Mya.

Europasaurus was a plant eater.

Professor Pete says:
Over a period of time animals can evolve into smaller animals called dwarf species. This can happen where food is scarce and there are no large predators.

Mamenchisaurus means 'Mamenchi lizard', from the place where the fossils were found in China.

Mamenchisaurus might have moved at the pace of a slow jogger, 12.8 kilometres per hour.

Mamenchisaurus was about 21–25 metres in length and weighed around 11 tonnes.

It lived in China during the Upper Jurassic period, 160–145 Mya.

Mamenchisaurus was a plant eater. Its spoon-shaped teeth were not for chewing, but were used like a rake to strip leaves off plants.

Mamenchisaurus

mah-MEN-chi-sore-us

Mamenchisaurus is known for having a very long neck. Like Diplodocus it may have used its long neck to feed on plants where the heavy dinosaurs could not go.

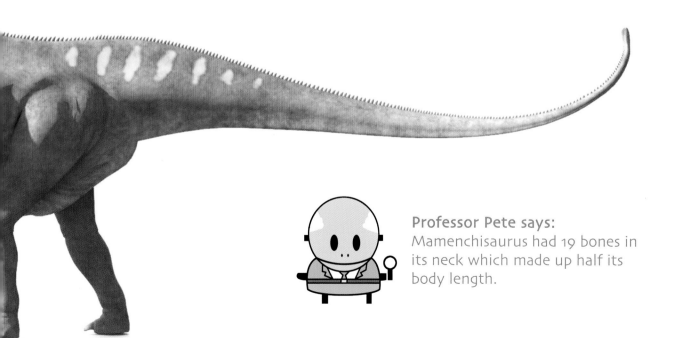

Professor Pete says:
Mamenchisaurus had 19 bones in its neck which made up half its body length.

Spinophorosaurus

SPY-no-FOR-oh-sore-us

This long-necked
dinosaur was unusual.
It had a pair of spikes at
the end of its tail. It used
them to defend itself
against attacks from
large predators.

Spinophorosaurus ate vegetation.

 It lived in Niger, Africa during the Middle Jurassic period, 176–161 Mya.

 Spinophorosaurus was 13 metres in length and 8.2 tonnes in weight.

 Spinophorosaurus was more agile than other sauropods and probably moved faster, up to 24 kilometres per hour.

 Spinophorosaurus means 'spine-bearing lizard' because of its tail spikes.

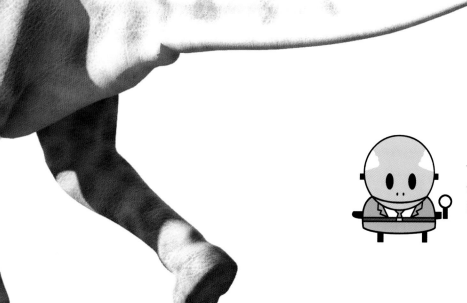

Professor Pete says:
The tail spikes on the end of the tail are called thagomizers by paleontologists.

21

Uberabatitan

OO-beh-RAH-bah-tie-tan

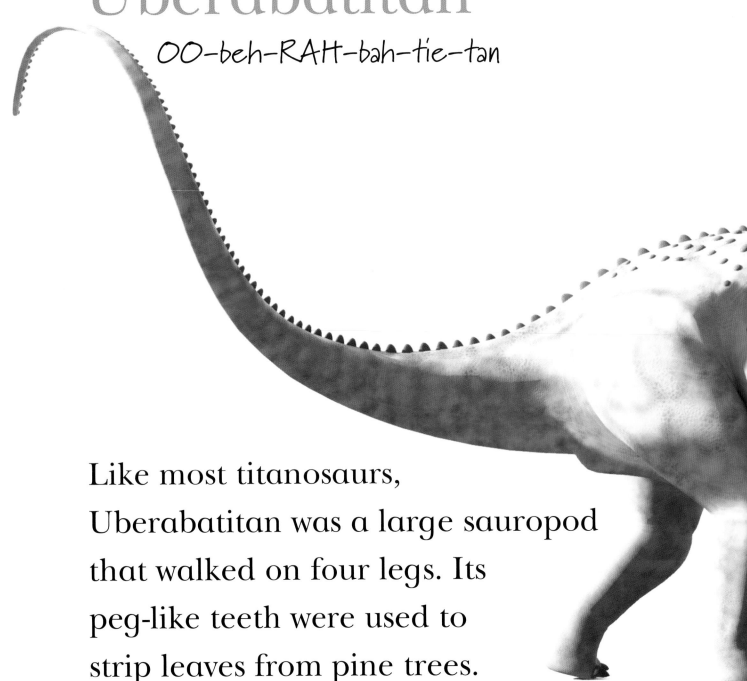

Like most titanosaurs,
Uberabatitan was a large sauropod
that walked on four legs. Its
peg-like teeth were used to
strip leaves from pine trees.

Uberabatitan ate plants.

 It lived in Brazil during the Upper Cretaceous period, 70–65 Mya.

 It measured up to 15–17 metres long, and weighed up to 11–15 tonnes.

 Uberabatitan might have been able to reach a top speed of 16 kilometres per hour.

 Uberabatitan was named after where it was found in Uberaba, in Brazil.

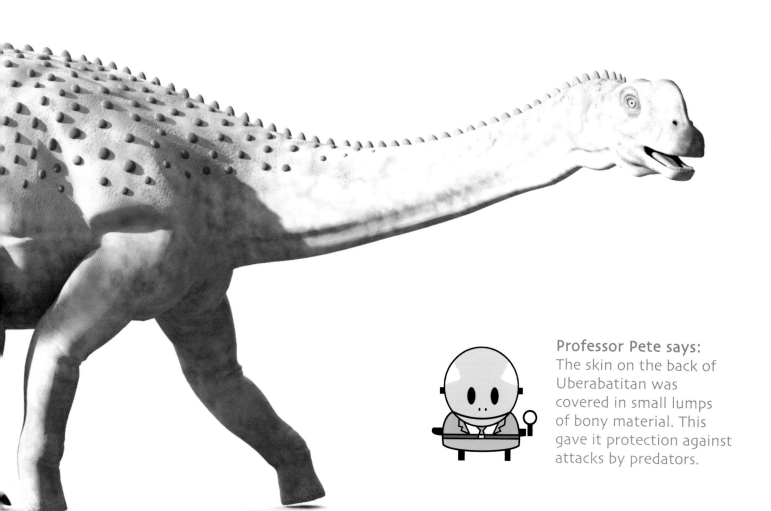

Professor Pete says:
The skin on the back of Uberabatitan was covered in small lumps of bony material. This gave it protection against attacks by predators.

Glossary

paleontologist
A scientist who studies early forms of life, chiefly by studying fossils.

predators
Animals that hunt and kill other animals for food.

sauropods
Long-necked, plant-eating dinosaurs.

titanosaurs
A group of long-necked dinosaurs that included some of the heaviest animals ever to walk the Earth.

Timeline

Dinosaurs lived during the Mesozoic Era which is divided into three main periods.

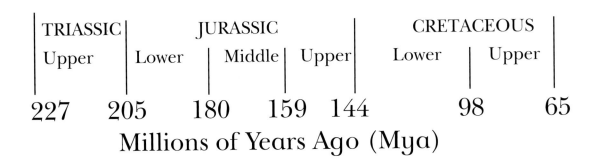

TRIASSIC	JURASSIC			CRETACEOUS	
Upper	Lower	Middle	Upper	Lower	Upper
227	205	180	159	144	98	65

Millions of Years Ago (Mya)